CHRISTMAS AROUND THE WORLD

Story by: **Astrid Anand**
Illustrations by: **Glick-Art**

Copyright © 2003 AM Productions
All rights reserved. Published in Canada by AM Productions
Ottawa-Canada (613) (745-3098)
Printed in India

It was the day before Christmas. The little village in the mountains of Panama* looked as drab as ever. There were no special lights or decorations anywhere. The villagers were just too poor. They went to midnight mass on Christmas Eve, but they did not give presents to their children. It was not their custom. As for Santa Claus, they had never heard of him and he had never come to their village.

Yet nobody seemed to mind, except the village schoolteacher. Her name was Maya Corazón. She wanted her students to celebrate the kind of Christmas that she had enjoyed as a child growing up in Panama City. And this year, on this day before Christmas, they would. They would because Miss Maya had finally arranged a Christmas party for her class, thanks to her brother's help. Her brother, Serafin, was as good as his name – an angel. At this very moment he was on his way, coming from Panama City to bring her everything she needed for the party.

But Miss Maya was keeping her plans a secret, until the afternoon. Since her students knew so little about Christmas celebrations, she needed to prepare them in advance for the surprise ahead. To do this she brought to school a book with a long title, but not too many words and lots of colored pictures in it. The name of the book was, "A Child's History of Christmas Around the World". As soon as the children had settled in their seats, she opened the book and began to read aloud.

The children sat spellbound, listening to every word. When the reading was over, each child had a turn to study the words and pictures more closely. I was there looking over their shoulders. This is what we learned.

*Panama is a long and narrow country. It is the 'isthmus' connecting Central and South America. Its most famous landmark is the Panama Canal, which links the two great oceans – the Atlantic and the Pacific – that lie on either side. Spanish is the official lanuage.

The most important Christmas story is 2000 years old. It tells us about the Nativity, the birth of Jesus in a stable in Bethlehem and the wonders surrounding his birth. The wonders are the sudden appearance of a brilliant star, angels rejoicing and the arrival of shepherds and three great kings to pay homage to the infant Jesus. The Nativity story has been told and retold in dozens of languages, in pictures that speak a thousand words, in musical concerts, in pageants and plays and in hand-crafted figures made of wood, stone, clay and other materials.

Our picture shows the holy infant lying in a manger, attended by his parents, Mary and Joseph, and the beasts of the stable. While no one knows exactly when he was born, Christians around the world have set aside December 25th as the day to celebrate and rejoice in the birth of Jesus,

According to the Christian calendar, twelve more days of Christmas follow the official birthday of Christ. The twelfth or last day, falling on January 6th, is often set aside as another special holiday called Epiphany or Three Kings Day. This day is marked to celebrate the coming of the three kings to Bethlehem. These same three kings are also known as the three wise men or *magi*. Together they followed the brilliant star and came to Bethlehem to honor Jesus as the newborn King of Kings, the Messiah, the Christ child. Each one, coming from a different land and having a different name, brought a precious gift. Melchior brought gold, Caspar brought sweet-burning frankincense, while Balthasar brought myrrh, a healing resin. Their gifts were the first Christmas presents. Since then, Christians all over the world celebrate the birth of Jesus by giving presents to their loved ones, especially their children.

The 2000 year old story of the Nativity and the coming of the three kings has inspired many new Christmas stories and traditions. At the center of all these new tales and traditions there is a figure who brings gifts to children. You will naturally think of Santa Claus, but his legend is a modern addition inspired by a much earlier source – the legend of Saint Nicholas.

The original Saint Nicholas was a real person. He was a fourth century Bishop of Myra (in present day Turkey) who was celebrated in his own lifetimes as a great friend and protector of children and the poor. For example, he saved three poor sisters from slavery when he secretly threw three bags of gold down the chimney of their house.

In many parts of Europe people celebrate his good deeds to this day. They set aside December 6th as Saint Nicholas Day, when they remember him by giving gifts to their children. In Germany the children call him *Nikolaus*, while the Dutch speaking children of Holland call him *Sinter Klaas*. For both he is the man with a full, white beard who carries a shepherd's crook, wears the red cape and miter (tall hat) of a bishop and brings them presents on the sixth of December.

Any child in Holland will tell you that *Sinter Klass* rides a white horse when he comes to visit them (while they are sleeping) on the night before Saint Nicholas Day. He travels with young Peter, who helps to distribute the presents. The presents are left in secret hiding places. In the morning the children search the house to find them. In the afternoon parents take their children downtown to watch the annual *Sinter Klaas* parade. Many different floats and attractions pass by, but the parade always ends with the arrival of *Sinter Klaas* himself. He comes mounted on a splendid, white horse to mingle with the crowds of cheering children. Young Peter, his helper, walks by his side.

In some parts of Germany the gift-bringer is not Saint Nicholas, but the *Chirstkindl*, that is to say, the Christ child himself. Children are told that on Christmas Eve the *Christkindl*, traveling on a white donkey, comes to bring them presents. A peasant, named *Ru Klaus*, travels with the holy child and helps to distribute the gifts. They go about their work secretly, while the children are fast asleep. Before they go to bed, the children set out baskets of hay for the donkey to eat. In the morning the hay is gone and they find presents of candy, clothing and toys inside the baskets. Today, when most people live in cities and towns, this tradition is seen as old-fashioned. Today, *Nikolaus* (Saint Nicholas) and the *Weihnachtsmann* (Santa Claus) are the two most popular Christmas gift-bringers in Germany.

England has the tradition of *Father Christmas*. He is a gigantic figure who wears a rich, crimson robe lined and trimmed with white fur. His head is crowned with evergreen plants such as holly, ivy or mistletoe, as a reminder in the depths of winter of the coming of spring. This red-robed giant is also one of the figures who visits Scrooge in Dickens' famous story, "A Christmas Carol". Today, *Father Christmas* can still be seen taking part in mummers' plays at Christmas time, where he shares the stage with knights and dragons and damsels in distress. As a gift-giver, he has lost his appeal. Much more appealing to children in England today is a small, kindly, red-cloaked Santa Claus figure who comes down the chimney on Christmas Eve to fill their stockings with presents – a feat that a giant like *Father Christmas* could never accomplish!

The tradition of bringing a fir tree into the house and decorating it for Christmas has its own story. It is a tradition at least 400 years old that probably started in Germany. The evergreen fir tree is a symbol of everlasting life. The candles and lights, decorating the tree, shine to remind us of the love Jesus had for the world. The star at the very top of the tree is to remind us of the star that announced the birth of Jesus. A crèche, that shows the Nativity scene, is often placed under the tree along with brightly wrapped Christmas presents. In Sweden girls wear a crown of evergreen branches and candles on December 13th, Saint Lucia's Day, as a symbol of hope, joy and light in the winter darkness. In some parts of Italy *Santa Lucia* is a gift-bringer. Italian children, who celebrate her special day, open *Santa Lucia's* gifts on December 13th.

The traditional gift-bringer in Sweden is the Christmas gnome, *Jultomten* (*Jul* is the Swedish word for Christmas, or Yule). On Christmas Eve children leave bowls of porridge for him to eat. Then they go to bed and he comes to visit them. In the morning they find his presents under the tree. The grown-ups must have seen *Jultomten*: they know how he looks. He is a gnome with a long, white beard and a red, pointed hat who travels with a goat. The goat carries a big bag of *julklappar* (Christmas "loot") on his back. In Finland it is *Joulupoukki* who brings presents on Christmas Eve. He rides a sleigh pulled by one reindeer and looks a lot like Santa Claus. Unlike Santa Claus, or other Christmas gift-givers, he does not come secretly. He visits the children at home while they are awake and delivers his gifts in person!

In Italy, in and around the city of Rome, the gift-bringer is the good witch Befana. She brings her gifts on the eve of Epiphany (the night before January 6th). Her legend recalls for us the Nativity and the coming of the three kings. *Befana's* story is this: the three kings stopped by her house on their way to Bethlehem; they asked her to come along, but she was too busy cleaning her house to join them right away. Ever since then, on Epiphany Eve, she flies from house to house on a broomstick with a sack of toys on her back. Flying in an out of the chimneys, she leaves her presents in the shoes of sleeping children, in case one of them is the Christ child. In Russia the same story is told of an old woman, *Babushka*, who must roam the world with her basket of toys in search of the baby Jesus.

In Portugal, in Spain and in most Latin American countries the three kings themselves are the gift-bringers. In preparation for their coming children leave their shoes by the door on the eve of Epiphany. While they are sleeping, the three kings arrive on foot with their gifts. In the morning the children wake up to find their shoes overflowing with candies and small toys. Later in the day the children flock downtown to see the annual Three Kings Day parade. All the floats are richly decorated, especially the last one on which the three kings ride. In the middle stands *Melchior*, the white-bearded king of ancient Nubia. He wears a golden crown. On either side of him stand *Caspar*, the youngest king, costumed in Turkish splendor and *Balthasar*, the Ethiopian king, dressed in a costume decorated with jeweled clasps.

Finally, we come to the newest Christmas gift-bringer, Santa Claus. He is the North American version of Saint Nicholas, a version first made popular in a poem written by Clement C. Moore and published in 1823. You probably know the opening lines: "Twas the night before Christmas when all through the house, Not a creature was stirring, not even a mouse." The poem goes on to describe "Saint Nick" as plump, jolly old elf. Since then the name has become Santa Claus – borrowed from *Sinter Klaas*, the name for Saint Nicholas that early Dutch settlers brought to America.

Santa Claus is a jolly old man with a white beard, a round belly, a red suit trimmed with white fur and a matching red cap. He visits children on Christmas Eve, when he flies around the world in a sleigh loaded with toys and pulled by eight reindeer. While the children are fast asleep, he flies from house to house with his team. Santa lands on the rooftops and climbs down the chimneys with presents from his sack. He leaves these presents under the Christmas tree or slips them into stockings that hang from the mantle piece. Then he glides up the chimney again to continue his round. When the long night is over, Santa Claus flies back to the North Pole, where he lives and his workshops are located. His workshops are staffed by elves, who make the toys he brings.

This version of Santa Claus – the ageless, white-bearded man in the red suit who gives out gifts to children on Christmas Eve and returns to his home at the North Pole – is now popular with children all over the world. In Spain he is called *Papa Noël*; in France, *père Noël*; in Italy, *Babbo Natale*; in Germany, *Weihnachtsmann*; in Japan, *Santa Kurohsu*; and the list goes on. Children everywhere love "Santa" a lot.

Let's go back to the schoolhouse in the mountains of Panama where the children are now well prepared to enjoy the teacher's surprise.

"Are you ready for my big Christmas surprise?" Maya Corazón asked her class.

"Yes, Miss Maya, we are ready!" the children exclaimed in a chorus.

The teacher walked to the back of the room. She was almost at the door when suddenly, it flew open on its own and a small procession marched in. The children were amazed to see Luiz, the carpenter come in, followed by Esmeralda, the school cook and then Juana, her assistant. Luiz carried his stepladder on one shoulder and a coil of rope on the other. Esmeralda marched in with her sleeves rolled up, as usual, but instead of carrying a pot of soup, she held a big piñata in her arms. The piñata – made of many layers of paper and paste – was molded into the shape of a Christmas tree and painted in a rainbow of colors. Juana, who brought up the rear, juggled many glasses of juice on a tray. Still, she managed to kick the door shut behind her before joining the others at the front of the class.

All at once the dumbfounded children found their voices. They jumped to their feet and cried with delight, "It's a party! It's a party!" As they crowded around Luiz, they urged him to hang up the piñata. So up the ladder he went. As soon as he was done, he proclaimed, "Let the party begin!" Then all the children clapped and cheered and rushed to join in the fun.

The children took turns trying to hit the piñata with a stick. It was not so easy. The players were blindfolded and sometimes Luiz pulled the piñata out of reach, making it even harder to hit the target. All the players got dizzy trying. But they did not give up. They laughed until their sides ached and took more turns. Finally, the piñata cracked wide open. An avalanche of candies and chocolates, wrapped in glittering foil, spilled across the floor. The players pushed back their blindfolds and everybody scattered here, there and everywhere to scoop up the sweets and eat them.

The children were busy licking chocolate from their fingers and drinking juice when suddenly they heard the tramp-tramping of boots on the roof. The noise soon stopped and for a moment all was still. Then they heard somebody shout, "Open the trap door!"

There was such a door in the roof, but it was used to let in air and light, not people. So who was up there now wanting to come in? Luiz climbed up the ladder to find out.

From the top of the ladder he eased the trap door open, poked his head outside and surveyed the flat roof. When he drew his head back in, he had this to report to the children below: "It's a man with a white beard, in a red suit, carrying a heavy sack. Should I let him come in?"

A chorus of eager voices shouted back, "Yes, let him in, let him in! It's Santa Claus! He has come to visit us!"

They were absolutely right. It was Santa Claus. He came down the ladder and stood in their midst. How wonderful he looked – like the picture in Miss Maya's book! More wonderful still, he spoke to them in Spainsh. "Feliz Navidad!" he cried, as he wished them all a Merry Christmas. Then he sat down in the teacher's chair and summoned the children by name, from a list. One by one, Santa gave each child a present from his sack. When the sack was empty, he said, "Now I must be on my way to visit other children, before I return to the North Pole. Please close your eyes and count to 100. When you open them, I will be gone. But I promise, I will visit you again next Christmas Eve."

The children were sad that he was leaving them so soon, but they did as they were told. When they opened their eyes, he was gone.

The first Christmas party they had ever had was over. However, before going home, they asked to see again the picture of Santa Claus in Miss Maya's book.

Camilo, who was never shy to speak his mind, declared, "Miss Maya, this is not a good picture of Santa Claus. He doesn't have a pink face and blue eyes; he has a brown face and dark eyes."

The teacher laughed. "You know, you are absolutely right," she said.

When Miss Maya came home, her brother, Serafin, was in the kitchen waiting for her. He had taken off his red coat and hat and pulled off his white beard. They were hanging on the chair beside him. Maya gave him a big hug of thanks. Then she repeated Camilo's clever remark to him.

Serafin laughed aloud. Still chuckling, he patted his sister's hand and said, "Now dark-eyed Santa has a surprise for the teacher. He's taking her home to Panama City for a Christmas family reunion. His van is parked outside. Luiz knows all about it. Tomorrow he'll post a sign on the school door: 'Closed for the twelve days of Christmas'. So pack your bag. We leave tonight."